Internat

M000196957

VOLUME 44 | 2021

EDITOR

Ana Hontanilla, UNC Greensboro

TRANSLATION EDITORS

Tia Nutters, Utrecht U and U of Groningen. Dutch
Michelle Cheyne, UMass Dartmouth. French
Rose Facchini, UMass Dartmouth. Italian
Darío Borim, UMass Dartmouth. Portuguese
Sarah Booker, UNC-Chapel Hill. Spanish

POETRY EDITORS

Mercer Bufter
Peter Dola, UNC Greensboro
Mark Smith-Soto, Emeritus, UNC Greensboro

FOUNDING EDITOR

Evalyn Pierpoint Gill

WEBSITE MANAGER

Joshua Lunsford

Founded in 1975 by Evalyn Pierpoint Gill, *International Poetry Review* is dedicated to the idea that the world becomes a better place when we continue to explore and listen to the voices of writers in diverse languages and from different cultures. This journal publishes works by contemporary writers in all languages, with facing English translations. *International Poetry Review* is of interest to anyone who loves the rhythms and beauty of the written word.

Acknowledgements

International Poetry Review would
like to acknowledge the following
lifelong supporters:

Louis Bourne
Phil Cohen
Fred and Susan Chappell
Bernhard Frank
Alice Hill
Ruthie Katzenstein
Stevenson Lupton, Jr.
Karol Neufeld
David Schenck, Ph.D.
Maria H. Schilke
Dr. Alan E. Smith
David and Zita Smith
Mrs. Betty Watson

The *International Poetry Review* is published annually by the Department of Languages, Literatures, and Cultures at UNC Greensboro. The journal was previously published twice a year through Volume 42, Numbers 1 & 2 (Spring & Fall 2016).

Authors who would like to publish their work in English translation and translators who would like to publish their work, please email the editor, Ana Hontanilla, at amhontan@uncg.edu. Please do not send manuscripts by mail.

Annual subscriptions for individuals are available through the Department for $14. A $8 international shipping fee will be added for non-U.S. subscribers. To subscribe, call (336) 334-5655 or email amhontan@uncg.edu. Institutions can subscribe through EBSCO or other agencies for $16.

International Poetry Review is also available on demand for $16. A $8 international shipping fee will be added for non-U.S. non-subscribers.

ISSN 1063-9128

Cover image: © Chema Castelló / Cucús / Stockholm, 2003

Typesetting: Ignacio López Alemany

UNC
GREENSBORO
Department of
Languages, Literatures,
and Cultures

Table of Contents

Letter from the Editors

Angles, Perspectives, Stories

The 44th issue of *International Poetry Review* (*IPR*) appears in a year shaped by change, social and political tensions. Social distancing has frustrated our human need for sociability, contact, and interaction, but has also gifted some of us with time for introspection. Our peer reviewers and members of the editorial team selected submissions that reflect a vast diversity of experiences, voices, and tones. The poems and translations cover themes such as the passage of time, the fragility of life, nature, the choices we confront and the ones that elude us, and the need for social justice and recognition. They also reflect a broad range of experiences and emotions, including separation, fear, and anger.

Hasheemah H. Afaneh describes the "posters and protests" that have woven through the streets of many Arab countries since 2010. UNCG undergraduate poet Karis Taylor explains with courage and solid arguments why pride is at the core of being Black. Viviana Paletta encourages the reader to look deeper into national landscapes, as some contain an "entourage of migrants/with no burials." Luis Correa-Díaz connects emotions, poetry, and social media while celebrating political change. Our team also sought submissions describing cultural experiences of exclusion associated with gender, race, age, nationality, language, and reduced mobility. Cindy King elaborates on the fear of invisibility felt by women who do not conform to western standards of beauty, Marta Sanz explores the fear of never being desired, and Noemi Alfieri writes about the consequences of not belonging to the fabric of the nation.

We thank members of the Association of Women Writers and Illustrators (AMEIS, Madrid, Spain) for their willingness to work with *IPR* on this issue. Founded in 2018, AMEIS focuses on providing visibility, opportunities, and access for women readers and creative writers. This organization advocates for women writers' equal representation and presence at conferences, festivals, and literary juries. By offering a space to play, discuss, and collaborate with Carola Aikin, Sonia Aldama, Isabel Cienfuegos, Carmen Peire, and Carmen Vega, who among others contributed to this volume through AMEIS, Issue 44 aims to bring the creative process closer to writers who feel excluded from the literary scene.

More words of appreciation are in order. I congratulate Mónica Gabriel y Galán on the publication of her latest book of poems. Thanks, too, to Rodrigo Montera for allowing himself to become vulnerable by virtue of publishing his poems with us, and to Marta Sanz for her inspiring words: "las mujeres nos estamos pensando" (women are rethinking ourselves). After a three-year hiatus, last year's *IPR* issue 43 was published thanks to the poets and translators who renewed their relationships with us; the University of North Carolina at Greensboro's Department of Languages, Literatures, and Cultures; and UNC Press.

I thank this year's peer reviewers for their insights, as well as Sarah Booker, Michelle Cheyne, Rose Facchini, and Tia Nutters for their work editing the translations and providing feedback to the numerous manuscript draft versions. Although every issue includes a limited number of works written in English, *IPR* publishes literature in translation; it is our mission to build pathways to hear voices in different languages. We are particularly thankful for the opportunity to include in this issue Dutch and Romanian contributions as well as bilingual poems in Arabic/English and Spanish/English.

Against the backdrop of the transformative events of 2020-2021, this issue underscores the role poetry plays in building communities. By structuring *IPR* around the core principles of empathy, solidarity, inclusion and accessibility, our goal is to become intentional about the capacity of language to enact change. By transforming experiences into poetic language, by translating a poem from one language to another, we enter into a dialogue with self and others; we bring together what is familiar and foreign. The editorial committee hopes that the poems included here make poetry accessible, move readers to play with words, and inspire them to become writers and translators themselves.

Ana Hontanilla, UNC Greensboro

Michelle Cheyne, UMass Dartmouth

Het raadsel *

Poem by Anna Enquist

Tijd heeft mij op de tuinbank neergezet,
een soplap in mijn hand gelegd. Toen
ik niet keek werd bloesem fruit,
hebben de wilgen zich verzilverd,
heeft het kind zijn eigen maaltijd
klaargemaakt.

Hij ziet ons zitten bij de vijgeboom,
wij lieten het konijn los in de tuin.
Het kind is achttien, wringt zijn hart
uit van verlangen en begrijpt niet
hoe hij hier kan blijven, hoe hij hier is
losgeraakt.

Verniel de haag, verzaag de stam,
vertrap de rozen, breek. Ik veeg
de spiegel schoon: nieuw gras
met glazen bloemen, jonge ouders
met hun kleine zoon, door tijd niet
aangeraakt.

* This poem was originally published in *Klaarlichte dag* (1996).

The Mystery

Translation by Arno Bohlmeijer

Time has placed me on the garden bench,
put a cleaning cloth in my hand. When
I was not looking, blooms became fruit,
the willows have grown silvery,
with care the child has prepared
his own meal.

He can see us by the fig tree,
we let the rabbit run free in the yard.
The child is eighteen, wringing his heart
from craving, and failing to understand
how he may stay here, how he came
to be detached.

Destroy the hedge, saw down the trunk,
trample the roses, break. I clean
the mirror: a new lawn
with glass flowers, young parents
with their little son, untouched
by time.

De diepe betekenis *

Poem by Leo Vroman

Ik sta wankelend aan de rand
van de Ware Diepe Betekenis
te staren of er een teken is
van de rare overkant,

en voel in mijn voeten de weeë lust
om die luchtzee maar in te springen.
De plons. De spreidende ringen.
Maar dit is geen kust.

Het is weer maandag vandaag.
We hebben het bed afgehaald,
weer een zakdoekje gevonden,

ik vraag 'Koffie?' zij zegt weer 'Graag',
en ik denk weer 'Dit is bepaald
alweer niet mijn laatste seconde.'

* This poem was originally published in *Nee, nog niet dood* (2008).

The Deeper Meaning

Translation by Arno Bohlmeijer

Reeling, I'm on the brink
of the True Deep Meaning,
peering to see if there's a sign
from the weird side across,

and in my feet I feel the feeble wish
to leap into the sky sea here.
The plunge. The widening rings.
But this is no shore.

Once more it's Monday today.
We're making the bed again,
finding another handkerchief,

"Coffee?" I ask, again she says, "Yes,"
and once more I reflect, "Yet again
it's definitely not my last second."

Love in the Time of Protests

Poem by Hasheemah H. Afaneh

After Gabriel Garcia Marquez

201-

High school crush posts a status updating us
on what we're constantly being updated on:
what is Egypt. . .Syria. . .and next will be Palestine,
and what is *how romantic, he knows politics,* swoon
like every Arab boy in the Arab world.
Share the status and update us on
whether he's noticed you have something in common
like every other Arab not living in a black hole.

201-

Learn that جنازة turns into a protest
before the dirt sets on the body,
or rather, the earth welcomes the body,
reminding us we came from her well before
we came from our mothers.
We protest death because we love our mothers.

201-

Airports and everywhere else are where
words get caught in the middle,
right between the Middle East and the West,
just like every bilingual's Arabic verb ends with an *ing,*
but this explanation is only the beginning.

Suggestion in grad school that the People
—yes, with a capital *P*—
protest harsh living conditions
was met with gasps of
how, why, but that's not realistic
because Spring is only spring break here.
My عيبر smells of flowers
mixed with tear gas.
And this is before I have an article in my inbox about
Israeli soldiers and PTSD interventions,
and the end of the occupation is not an intervention,
and I meet this with gasps for air.

201-

Meant to tell you this
somewhere
      between
you explaining what life was like
on a military base
      and
myself explaining what life is
           in the midst of   a military occupation
that would never occupy your mind
unless you think of me when I leave and bring you back olives
for your martini
—but my olives are too sacred for a martini—
I need you to taste them raw, next to زيت و زعتر.

201-

Imagine that
we're on the same side
and that you're an ally,
so when I fall in the عيبر

you'll grab me by the arm
        and
not let me   go
because I'll tell you ملنا ش غير بعض
which means *we only have each other,*
        or
        one another.

201-

So,
if I fell in love with anyone not Arab,
would we raise our sons to say
ملنا ش غير بعض
or
we only have each other
or
will they be somewhere
        between
spring and ربيع؟

Take the Plastic Chairs

Poem by Hasheemah H. Afaneh

Do we grab the plastic chairs from outside
   and go inside, or
Do we grab the plastic chairs from inside
   and go outside,
Which revolution do we go after,
   and what's timing got to do with it?
Posters and protests are woven through the streets,
 and the songs start from our doorstep, leaving no sound behind.
Our "List the 50 States" game in English
   becomes List the Martyr's Squares in Arabic.
It's not a game that'll depend on how many martyrs,
   but you'll need to tell which city, which Ahmad, which
Dar Abu
Which plastic chairs do we put
   under our protest tents in Ramallah, Tripoli, Cairo?
They tell you to take them back inside,
   or they'll flip them—and you—on their heads.
Those plastic chairs are our *sahrat*,
   and nights on the *baranda*,
   and afternoons between the pomegranate and lemon trees,
            and
            and
            and

Remember when we decided to put the plastic chairs outside
   after we heard about the earthquake coming,
   and we planted them on the cement in front of the settlement,
   as if guarding it with our lives.
The earthquake never came,
        but the revolution did.

Swaying to National Anthems

Poem by Hasheemah H. Afaneh

My body sways to Mawtini and I think of how watan is
 Sidi singing
 and
 Siti laughing
not knowing
that her husband of decades
knew the words by heart,
and my body sways to Mawtini
as I try to remember
 if Mawtini was borrowed
 or
 if Mawtini was written
for a nation that craved an anthem
 to rise to,
after those that fell in the uprisings.

   My body fights me when the National Anthem
    plays in football stadiums,
     or
    plays during graduation ceremonies
   and I want
    to sit
    instead
     of standing on command
  as their bodies sway and mine stiffens
    in the heat of the rage of their sea-blue
  eyes
    as they wonder why your body
does not sway like theirs.

We

Poem by Alan Cohen

The bees sing oboe in the Indian hawthorn
A song of honey, sleep and threat

On a day so still, no leaf stirring
The shimmering fountain makes the only other sound
(Like a night of so few lights, we can see the Milky Way again)

The Joseph's coat climbing rose
Two thirds up the trellis
Clothed in 50 roses, still harboring 30 buds
And I sit under our fancy wrought iron gazebo
(Pause: not a single bird has sung or shown itself in an hour)

When we arrived, five years ago, the entire yard was dried mud
We might have planted vegetables
Put in pool, grill, tennis court, hot tub
We chose a flower garden
(Now maturing, in mid-April, mid-Spring)

What we choose, what we see
What we know, what we believe
What we want, is, for every one of us, unique
Here, today, the scent of jasmine, of lemon blossom on the air
(Ah, here comes the jay now, proud, belly white, in for a drink)

Museum

Poem by Stuart Gunter

> for Kehinde Wiley, Marcus-David Peters, and George Floyd

I walk up to the locked doors in the drizzling rain,
try to get in. I turn to the Chihuly reeds
alongside the building, then wander
over the gravel courtyard to *Rumors of War.* Folks
up on Monument Avenue celebrating Juneteenth
at Marcus-David Peters Memorial Park, playing
basketball, grilling hot dogs. There is a band. All
in the shadow of Lee's statue. Traveler was
too small for the sculptor, who chose to use a different
horse. My friend is writing a song about this,
from the horse's point of view, as a slave.
That evening, the image of George Floyd looks
on the people in the grass, his image emblazoned
in lights on the graffitied, spray-painted plinth.

Daily Affirvotions

Poem by Cindy King

Those pains in your chest aren't a heart attack, it's that bra you've
been wearing since high school.

No, you're not fat, your friend's just built like a runway model.

That face you glimpsed in the storefront window, don't worry, it
wasn't yours (and of course they sell those jeans in your size).

You look old in that picture only because you're holding a
newborn. But no, no worries, that baby's not yours.

You're not pregnant for at least five different reasons. And certainly
not, no, not one of them is menopause.

That's just a pimple, a hangnail, an ordinary mole.

Did you forget, you left your place a mess? No, you haven't been
burglarized.

No one has used your credit card in El Paso; no one's charged a
slushy, a Slim Jim, and 50 cartons of Winstons.

Yes, you spellchecked that message, changed *shits* to *shirts* before
clicking send. And that letter, yes, it had plenty of postage; the
receiver has just chosen not to reply.

Your car is in park, parking brake on. It has not rolled through the
garage door, down the driveway, and out into the quiet street. No,
your headlights aren't on.

Those are white hydrangeas, not doctors staked in the bushes. No, that's a unicorn, not a police car.

Relax, no one's looking at you. That fine young gentleman's not staring, he sees right through, to the unicorn standing behind you,

and as for God, as for God you're good, God doesn't see you either.

My Father's Helmet

Poem by Tim Mayo

In the trunk in the attic of my father's
imaginary house, I reach with both hands
and lift out his lead-scarred helmet,
the one, which, each day of his war,
protected his hopes and fleeting dreams
from combat's most irreparable harm.

I look deep into the olive-drab darkness,
where the air holds its vacant wisdom,
then place the helmet on my head,
and in that silent surge of armor,
the past I supposed becomes apparent
and I begin to think like my father.

I begin to smell the same rat-like fear
which curled like smoke in his nostrils
on the last day he wore it. I begin to feel
the staccato tap of death slamming his head
down, hear its leaden pings & splats
as it caroms off the helmet's metal shell.

I can even see the same daffodils he saw,
their sunlit heads bobbing & weaving
outside a machine gun's line of fire, waving
beside the slit-smile of the gray, hive-shaped nest,
where the gunner spits out his bullets like furious
bees searching to sting anything that moves.

I see, now, desperate for life, he had no choice
but to cradle the emptiness of it in his arms,
to crawl that perilous distance toward daffodils
and my mother's bed, praying he could shed

along the way fear's useless skin,
while, above, the bees searched the air.

I see, I too, must make myself that humble
as I enter this faraway cemetery, move toward
those yellow blossoms some stranger--kin?--
has placed before my father's gray headstone,
where I finally kneel to place this offering,
this armored knowledge I can never pierce.

Here Comes the Sun

Poem by Gordon E. McNeer

For Richard Brautigan

Every morning
I wake up to these words
and the music of the dead
reaches out to me.

Yeah, you gotta enjoy
these moments
before they come to an end:
these sunrises,
as magnificent as they are,
once lit up the eyes
of John Lennon,
and those sunsets
that await you in the evening
caused the soul to vibrate
of Charles Baudelaire.

Every day we are diminished
in our own way.
If you are lucky, there will be
a moment in your day
that you will share with Buddy Holly.
If you are lucky, Mark Twain
will cast you a line
as his riverboat fades away.

I am old but fortunate:
as of yet, I have not heard
the unmistakable sound

of a single action Colt
inviting me to dream
in watermelon sugar
where the deeds will be done
once and forever
and tigers sleep beneath the river
as moonlight plays on the banks
of the town of Ideath.

Richard, what was that moment like,
when everything inside of you was broken,
when the wine glasses of dawn
had not yet spoken to you,
when the first rays of the sun brought
Luis Buñuel's razor opening
the mind's eye in the mirror,
when the darkness settled about you
like Rimbaud's vision of hell,
and you found yourself waiting alone
in the darkness for the words
of John, Paul, George and Ringo Starr.

Upon coming across a picture of my friend Nancy with her younger son, the year she died

Poem by David Schenck

i.

damn the buddha
screw sakyamuni

there is no way
there is no way

do not tell me
"suffering is optional"

two decades gone, i
crumble to nothing.

no fine monk, my seat
can't hold this sorrow.

there is no way
there is no way

no balancing, no
no squaring karma

still seared, wrenched
i refuse to let her go.

ii.

courageous, generous
to the universe + us all–

far more lovely a spirit
than I can muster now

except when I feel
her touch, just here–
her hand over mine,
her tears over mine.

"don't grieve me
this way—don't."
oh, but I can
find no other—

"come then,
let me hold you
against the night."

iii.

the monks say,
"talk is ego"—
but ego comforts
not, only evades.
these words, then,
something other.

come to minister
to my heart—or
perhaps they are
the heart, breaking
through, breaking up,
breaking back to her.

iv.

the mountains will
not reproach me

tomorrow. they do not
reproach us now.

for now, they tower
in the darkness, silent
unmoving—waiting.

tomorrow they will
celebrate, as ever—
and pour their joy
over us both.

"come, little man—
don't be a fool!
even the dead girl
says you should sing."

My Ode to Black Women

Poem by Karis Taylor

If you have ever been told that you are not good enough
If you ever have been questioned for what you can bring to the table
If your voice has ever been neglected in order to support someone else's view
Seen as less than, simply due to the color of your skin
Then this is for you.

Black women
Let it be known that despite everything being thrown at us
We are still standing tall on the foundation of hate they built for us
We are beautiful; our beautiful dark skin, brown skin, light skin
can endure any pressure they put on us
We are the example
We are the trend
We are the innovators
We are the leaders
Black women, they try to shut down your voice because once you speak you are too powerful to stop
Black women, we must know our worth
Or they will assume it for us.
They hate how we love our curls, the way we cherish our bodies, how intellectual we are
But then just as quickly mimic us like a moth imitates a butterfly
They see the treatment of Black women in this country
And still question why our lives matter

We are mothers, sisters, and daughters, humans who will sacrifice for those who we love but still suffer in silence with our hidden barriers
We are not, I repeat, We are not, Angry Black Women
But rather Impenetrable Black Women

Like the women before us
Harriet Tubman, Septima Clark, Coretta Scott King
To the women now
Michelle Obama, Toni Morrison, Mae Jemison
We are standing on the structure of their words, their actions,
their visions for a better tomorrow and a greater future
Say her name, say her name, say her name
Breonna, Sandra, DeCynthia, Hannah, Alteria, ShaAsia
A bus seat couldn't stop Rosa nor Claudette
Discrimination couldn't stop Dorothy
Racism couldn't stop Josephine
Black women, I see you
Black women, I hear you
Black women I love you
We will never stop saying your name
Black women
I hope you know that every type of criticism formed against you
will cease to exist
I hope you know that every day I will continue to lift your voice
I hope you know that you are worth more than how you view you
in this tainted society
And may we never stop being proud of our Blackness.

Masterchef

Poem by Irene Moccia

Nel forno dei giorni
arrostiti dal dolore patito,
la vera sfida:
restare morbidi.
Con fiducia amniotica
nella fertilità dell'acqua,
lasciare ai sogni
il tempo di lievitare,
crescersi senza seccare.

Poesia di non amore

Poem by Stefano De Vecchi

Ruberei la luna
ruberei l'altrui fortuna
per te
Sempre per te
ruberei gli altrui versi
dai miei tanto diversi
Tutto per te
ruberei
Non ti amo
e niente di mio
ti darei.

Masterchef

Translation by Rose Facchini

In the oven of time
roasted from the pain suffered,
the real challenge:
remaining flexible.
With amniotic confidence
in the fertility of water,
leave to dreams
the time to rise,
to grow without drying out.

Non-Love Poem

Translation by Rose Facchini

I would steal the moon
I would steal the luck of others
for you
Always for you
I would steal the verses of others
that are so different from mine
Everything for you
I would steal
I do not love you
and nothing of mine
would I give you.

Uma perturbadora intrusa

Poem by Noemi Alfieri

Tenho sido a estrangeira, alheia ao
corpo da nação. Enquanto, na hora mais escura,
andava pelos subúrbios de cidades desconhecidas
alguém gentilmente me sugeriu
para eu voltar para a minha terra. Naquele exato momento senti-me

sem medo

apesar de saber que estava ferida, fraca, sozinha
porque alheia também significa abusada,
    aprisionada,
        espancada. Por vezes a filha
de um passado oculto, que as pessoas tendem a obliterar. Aquela
que escolhe nuas palavras como ato de subversão

aquela que reescreve sua história. Não feminina,
porém mulher. Definidamente dissonante
a não ser que sintas a raiva dos outros, a não ser que a tua dor
te mantenha acordado, insomne.

Subversão

porque palavras sofisticadas nada significam para aqueles que
                             seguram
a vida a partir do nível do chão. A subcidade está longe
de salas de estar enfeitadas

Lá estou eu

Disturbing Intruder

Translation by Noemi Alfieri and Alexis Levitin

I've been the outsider, a stranger to
the body of the nation. While in the darkest hour
I wandered through the outskirts of unknown cities
someone kindly suggested that
I go back home. That very moment I felt

free of fear

though aware that I was broken, wounded, and alone
for the stranger also is the one abused,
      imprisoned,
            beaten down. Sometimes the daughter
of a hidden past, which people tend to blot from memory. The one
who chooses naked words as a subversive act,

the one who writes her history anew. Not feminine,
yet a woman. Definitely dissonant,
unless you feel the rage of others, unless their pain
fails to keep you sleepless, insomniac.

Subversion

for sophisticated words mean nothing to those who grasp
life from the level of the ground. The undercity, far
from brightly decorated living rooms

There am I

Deitada no passeio entre granadas
um suor frio cola as minhas mãos ao chão
porém vejo
montanhas brancas e ondas azuis.

Naquele segundo esqueço
Que fui abusada
aprisionada,
epsancada.

Muito mais do que cicatrizes sangrentas, no entanto
nunca ajustada às expectativas
essencialmente uma intrusa
uma semente que tardia floresce

Sem medo.

Lying on the pavement between grenades
my hands stuck by cold sweat to the ground
and yet I see
white mountains, blue waves.

In that moment I forget
that I have been abused
                imprisoned
                        beaten down.

Much more than bloody scars, yet
never fit for expectations,
essentially an intruder
        a seed, late-blossoming,

and free of fear.

Limbă calică de poet balcanic *

Poem by Nora Iuga

Iată-mă întinsă pîntec peste pîntec cu umbra mea
M-ar fi iubit Vallejo, m-ar fi iubit Jacques Brel
în joile lor de moarte şi primăvară
în camere de hotel cu cămăşi murdare şi cravate
atîrnînd ca ştreangul pe instinctul cabrat într-o ultimă foame
nu găsesc un burete să-mi şterg mirosul spermei lor
din creier, nu găsesc un dizolvant sigur
pentru aceste pete grase lăsate de ei
în degetele cu care scriu...
ah, limbă scurtă, limbă calică de poet balcanic
prea pudic organ mincinos impotent
cum de nu te scoate mizeria din propriii tăi dinţi
cum nu plezneşti de-atîta sete comprimată
de atîta dragoste de-atîta scîrbă
sînt o femeie întinsă pîntec peste pîntec cu umbra mea
m-ar fi iubit Vallejo m-ar fi iubit Jacques Brel
în această muţenie pestilenţială care încearcă să cînte...

Stingy Balkan Poet's Tongue

Translation by Victor Pambuccian

Here I am stretched womb upon womb with my shadow
Vallejo would have loved me, Jacques Brel would have loved me
on their Thursdays of death and springtime
in hotel rooms with dirty shirts and ties
hanging like a noose on the pranced instinct of a last hunger
I don't find a sponge to wipe off the smell of their sperm
from my brain, I don't find a sure-fire solvent
for the grease stains they left
on the fingers I write with ...
ah, short tongue, stingy Balkan poet's tongue
too chaste, a lying, impotent organ
how come the scum is not moving you out of your own teeth
how come you don't burst out of so much compressed thirst
out of so much love out of so much disgust
I am a woman stretched womb upon womb with my shadow
Vallejo would have loved me, Jacques Brel would have loved me
in this pestilential muteness that tries to sing ...

În spaţiul alb o mînă străină *

Poem by Nora Iuga

Dac-aş putea să-mi citesc poeziile
cu alţi ochi, nu cu ochii ăştia sentimentali
de vacă bătrînă
şi dacă aş putea recunoaşte
că bărbatul mort e piatra scoasă din vezica mea biliară
fără aceste două poveri esenţiale
m-aş regăsi iar liberă şi tînără
dar ce se petrece în spaţiul acela alb
cînd o mînă străină îţi smulge
din măruntaie un organ
care te chinuieşte de-o viaţă
semnalizîndu-ţi clipă de clipă
faptul "dureros de dulce" (Eminescu)
că trăieşti. e o grea dilemă aceasta
ca şi cum ceasul de la mîna mea
mi-ar vorbi despre secundele
care se întorc poţi să-l vezi?

* These poems were originally published in the Romanian literary
magazine *Viaţa Românească* (2018).

In the White Space a Foreign Hand

Translation by Victor Pambuccian

If I could read my poems
with other eyes, not with these sentimental eyes
of an old cow
and if I could admit
that the dead man is the stone taken out of my gallbladder
without these two essential burdens
I would find myself free and young again
but what happens in that white space
when a foreign hand pulls from
your entrails an organ
that kept tormenting you for a lifetime
signaling time and again
the "painfully sweet" (Eminescu) fact
that you live. this is a burdensome dilemma
as if the watch from my wrist
would talk to me about the seconds
that come back can you see it?

Georgia on My Mind, Reset in 2020

Poem by Luis Correa-Díaz

Georgia on my mind reset in 2020

aunque no vine al mundo
en este sur y aunque muera
en el que florecen copihues,
siempre estarás *on my mind*,
más ahora que has beaten
the odds, que *a song of you*
aroma dulcemente los cielos
de este país tan rojo y tan
azul como los temporales
de su bandera, *I said Georgia,*
oh Georgia —quién me trajo,
y se me llena el corazón
de una *paz* que sólo conocí
entre tus *brazos* y tus blessing
*moonlight*s over me, escuchando
a Gladys Knight & The Pips

Georgia on My Mind, Reset in 2020

Poem by Luis Correa-Díaz

Georgia on my mind reset in 2020

although I didn't come into the world
in this south and even if I die
where copihues bloom,
you'll always be *on my mind*,
more now that you've beaten
the odds, that *a song of you*
sweetly scents the skies
of this country so red and so
blue like the storms
battling its flag, *I said Georgia,
oh Georgia* —who brought me
here?—, and that fills my heart
with a *peace* I only got to know
in your *arms* and under your
sacred *moonlight*s listening to
Gladys Knight & The Pips

Saltamontes *

Poem by Carola Aikin

Érase una vez un saltamontes solitario que a la hora de la siesta
rascaba sus patitas y saltaba de un lado a otro de la blanca habitación.
Una habitación toda blanca, sí, menos por una cascada de cabellos
rojos, menos por unos párpados que se abren y descubren una
mirada de enredaderas. Entonces el saltamontes y aquella mirada
intiman como nunca hubieran imaginado.
-¿La beso? -duda el saltamontes.
-¿Me habré vuelto loca? -se pregunta la mujer.

* This poem was originally published in *Las escamas del dragón* (2005).

Nací en hilera de hormigas *

Poem by Sonia Aldama Muñoz

Nací en hilera de hormigas sobre un hueco de tierra crispada por las
cáscaras. Fui colonia de pájaros sin voluntad que buscaban semillas
para formar otra hilera; usurpé vergel, basura y barro, un sol quemó
la arcilla, la lluvia regó cada fruto, pero el viento sólo levantó ceniza.
Habité un enjambre de abejas, delirio que despojaba a la reina de
privilegios, fui miel y colmena, ausencia en revolución de hermanas
que migraban a otra prisión. Hoy vuelo roja en suburbio sin raíces,
desierto de agitación y de plegarias, gota a favor del aliento o tela
que araña tréboles sin hojas. Y resisto en el pecho la respiración de
voz mojada.

* This poem was originally published in the collection *Cuarto solo* (2013).

A Grasshopper at Naptime

Translation by Nadine Novack

Once upon a time there was a lonely grasshopper who at naptime rubbed his legs together and hopped from one side to the other of the white room. An all-white room, indeed, except for a cascade of red tresses, except for eyelids that open up and reveal a sight of ivy. And then the grasshopper and that gaze become as intimate as they would never have imagined.

"Should I kiss her?" the grasshopper wonders.

"Have I lost my mind?" the woman wonders.

I Was Born in a Line of Ants

Translation by Ana Grandal

I was born in a line of ants over a hollow in the earth nettled by the broken eggshells. I was a colony of birds devoid of will that sought seeds to build another line; I usurped the orchard, the waste, and the mud, a sun scorched the clay, the rain watered each fruit, but the wind only blew ashes. I dwelled in a swarm of bees, delirium that despoiled the queen of her privileges; I was honey and hive, absence in a revolution of sisters who migrated to another prison. Today I fly red in rootless suburb, desert of bustle and prayers, drop on behalf of spur, or web that scratches leafless clovers. And I bear in my chest the breath of the wet voice.

Paraíso

Poem by María Villa Cámara Gómez

Detrás de la Colina
La Casa de atrás
Allí se encuentra
El Paraíso

Emily Dickinson

Perder *se*
         entre pensamientos
que cavan zarzas entre aguas turquesas
que sostienen la niñez.
Ser Raíz que mama del árbol
que habita en este paraíso
que anhelas
acunando pájaros tatuados
en la piel de un viejo libro
que un niño desdentado
hojea entre el vacío de sus dedos.

¿Acaso no fui lluvia o escarcha?

¿Acaso no fui dolor que hirió tu piel ajada?

Paradise

Translation by Ana Grandal

> *Behind the Hill—the House behind—*
> *There—Paradise—is found!*
>
> *Emily Dickinson*

To lose *oneself*
                    amidst thoughts
that dig brambles among turquoise waters
that sustain childhood.
To be the Root that suckles the tree
that dwells in this paradise
you yearn for
rocking birds tattooed
on an old book's skin
that a toothless child
leafs through the emptiness between his fingers.

Wasn't I rain or frost?

Wasn't I pain that wounded your faded skin?

Naufragio

Short Story by Isabel Cienfuegos

Mi madre vuelve a perderse en el salón de casa, el pelo blanquísimo. Parece el hada de los imposibles, la maga del sinsentido. Nos tenemos que ir, dice. Por esa puerta, urge, y me señala la librería. Inútil argumentar que por allí no vamos a ninguna parte. Ella comienza a abrirse paso. Vuelan figuritas de loza. Nos despiden mis hermanos desde los retratos. Por ellos le suplico que pare. ¡No tengo hijos!, grita, vámonos de una vez. Zozobramos entre reproches y razonamientos. Intento evitar que se hunda, le sigo la corriente, nado con ella un buen rato. Alrededor nuestro, los libros que su furia arrancó flotan en un mar de desconsuelo. Tomo uno y comienzo a leer. Las palabras nos sostienen y nos llevan a una isla de cuento. Creo que estamos a salvo un día más.

Shipwreck

Translation by Carola Aikin and Nadine Novack

My mother gets lost again in the living room at home, her hair bright white. She looks like the fairy of impossibilities, the sorceress of nonsense. We must go, she says. Through that door, she urges, and she points at the bookshelves.

It's useless to argue that that way leads nowhere. She starts to make her way. Ceramic figurines fly everywhere. My siblings wave goodbye from their picture frames. For their sake I plead her to stop. I have no children! she yells, let's go once and for all.

We flounder among reproaches and reasonings. I try to prevent her from sinking, I go with the flow, I swim alongside her for a long while. Surrounding us, the books her fury tore out float in a sea of grief. I pick one up and begin to read. The words support us and carry us to a storybook island. I think we're safe for one more day.

Síndrome de Meniere

Poem by María Luisa Cortés

Nadie escucha la alarma sorda
resonar en la garganta.
Solo yo oigo el timbre.
Me desmorono.
El suelo choca mi cuerpo
tras un bucle y cinco piruetas.
Me levanto de nuevo,
y vuelvo a leer
palabras en los labios.
Me mancho de lágrimas
de carmín y media sonrisa,
de ecos que no descansan.

Meniere's Syndrome

Translation by Ana Grandal

No one hears the dull alarm
ringing in my throat.
Only I can hear the sound.
I fall apart.
The ground hits my body
after a spin and five pirouettes.
I stand anew,
and again I read
words on lips.
I stain myself with tears
of lipstick and half a smile,
with echoes that never rest.

La canción

Short story by Bárbara Darder

Acaban de tener sexo en la cama del hotel dónde han pasado la primera noche de casados. Aunque llevan tiempo conviviendo, no ha faltado un ramo de flores blancas en la mesa baja de la suite nupcial ni una botella de champagne. Ella espera. Después del coito, él acostumbra a pasarle una batería de preguntas. Quiere conocer su pasado, su presente y hasta su futuro. Una pareja sin secretos, quiere él. Pero hoy coge el mando para sintonizar un canal de música de la tele. Se escucha una canción. Déjala, le pide ella. No recuerdo el título de la canción, dice él. Y la mira con un gesto de interrogación. Ella no responde a la pregunta. No piensa decirle el título de la canción. Una canción que nunca olvidará. Un secreto al menos.

Un secreto que acaricia su cuerpo como carnosos pétalos de rosas cuando tiene sexo con él. No le dice que era la canción preferida de Carlos para estrecharla entre los brazos en la pista de baile, que bailaban con un ritmo que él no logra. Que ni siquiera los intenta o al menos eso le parece a ella. ¿Y si comprara el disco y al llegar a casa le pidiera que lo bailaran? ¿Podría apartar así de su mente al hombre que no consigue olvidar del todo? ¿Es buena idea bailar con el marido la canción del verano que la enamoró de otro? ¿Es buena idea recordar las manos alrededor de su cintura que acercaban los dos cuerpos, el calor del sexo del otro?

Necesita tiempo. Con el tiempo olvidará que ella, para Carlos, como mucho, fue la canción de un verano. Que regresó a la ciudad para casarse con la novia.

Olvidar. Para eso se ha casado.

Mira. Eso ¿Por qué te casaste conmigo? nunca se lo ha preguntado.

Olvidará la canción. Una canción no es nada, el título de una canción, menos que nada. ¿No recuerdas el título? insiste él, después de apagar la tele sin que la canción hubiera terminado.

The Song

Translation by Katelyn Smith

They just had sex in the hotel bed where they spent their first night as a married couple. Although they've lived together for a while, there is still a bouquet of white flowers and a bottle of champagne on the coffee table in their honeymoon suite. She waits. After intercourse, he usually proceeds with a battery of questions. He wants to know about her past, present, and future. A couple without secrets, that's what he wants.

But today he takes the TV remote and flips to a music channel. A song is playing. Leave it on, she pleads. I don't remember the name of the song, he says. And he gives her a probing look. She doesn't answer his question. She doesn't intend to tell him the name of the song. A song she will never forget. One secret, at least.

One secret that caresses her body like luscious rose petals when they have sex. She doesn't tell him that it was Carlos's favorite song to hold her in his arms on the dance floor to, that they danced to with a rhythm that her husband can't keep up with. He doesn't even try to, or at least, that's how she sees it. If they had bought the CD, would she have asked him to dance to it when they got home? Could she then rid her mind of the man she can't seem to forget? Is it a good idea to dance with her husband to a song from the summer when she fell in love with another man? Is it a good idea to remember those hands around her waist, their two bodies together, the heat of the other's sex?

She needs time. With time, she will forget that she was, for Carlos, at the very most, a song from a summer. That he went back to the city to marry his girlfriend.

To forget. That's why she got married.

Look. That "Why did you marry me?" was never asked.

She'll forget the song. A song means nothing, the name of a song, less than nothing. You don't remember the name? He insists, turning off the TV before the song could end.

Tic Tac *

Prose Poetry by Mónica Gabriel y Galán

"Tan solo dispone usted de doce minutos para abandonar su casa, la casa en la que vive con sus lámparas y radiadores, y llevarse un único objeto que conviva con usted el resto de sus días". Un susto me desata. Un regimiento de formas se agolpa queriendo pasar lista aunque nada falte y todo sobre en esta fatiga de los materiales. Me pregunto de qué sustancia tendrán que ser los tachones de mi valija, qué milagro es el que cabe en el cuero de mi saco capaz de franquear todas las aduanas. Tendrá que ser, al menos, opaco como la arena, subversivo como un sombrero, sin arrugas como las cucharas, más corto que mi antebrazo y tan necesario como un vaso de vino. Inevitablemente pasan los minutos. Sí, finalmente opto por dejar el reloj sobre la mesa.

La recomendación de un experto: *

Poem by Mónica Gabriel y Galán

Navegad interminablemente en alta mar aquellos cuyo color favorito sea el azul. El resto, abstenerse. Debido a la perversión del azul veríais la vida de color rosa.

Test de inteligencia *

Poem by Mónica Gabriel y Galán

¿Quién heredará la Tierra?

Un muchacho esférico al que no pueda tumbar un soplo.

* These poems were originally published in the collection *Con los ojos bien cerrados* (2020).

Tick-Tock

Name of translator not provided

"You have no more than twelve minutes to abandon your house, the house where you live, with its lamps and radiators, and take with you a single object that will accompany you for the rest of your life." I am startled. A regiment of forms crowds together for the roll call, though nothing is missing and everything is superfluous among this redundancy of things. I wonder about the composition of the tacks on my valise and about the miracle that would fit inside the leather of my bag, one that can pass through every Customs. At the very least, it should be lusterless like sand, subversive like a hat, unwrinkled like a spoon, no longer than my forearm, and as necessary as a glass of wine. Inevitably, minutes pass. Yes, in the end, I opt to leave the watch on the table.

Expert Recommendation:

Name of translator not provided

Those whose favorite color is blue should sail endlessly on the high seas. The rest, please abstain. Blue's perverse nature is such that you would see life tinted rosy.

Intelligence Test

Name of translator not provided

Who will inherit the Earth?

A spherical boy who cannot be knocked down by a breath of air.

El mal poema

Poem by Manuel Gahete

> *Vive en un barril.*
> *Pártete la cabeza con un hacha.*
> *Planta tulipanes bajo la lluvia.*
> *Pero no escribas poesía.*
>
> *Bukowski*

Quizás nos atrevemos
—quizás por enfrentarnos al infinito mundo—
       a ser de otra manera,
a dejarnos la piel del yo en el otro cuando guardamos celo de la muerte.
Somos tan indefensos bajo el tenso desnudo que nos labra,
bajo el tremor que ciega
los ríos de la sangre, la flor de tanto nervio cuya visión extraña nos adumbra.
Y sigues escribiendo amor como si nada,
como si el tiempo crudo que nos hurga y me deja tendido a la intemperie
no fuera más que olvido o más que sombra.
Dejarías seguro de escribirme cuando escribes amor si
comprendieras el dolor que destilan tus palabras,
el dolor que me cuesta recibirlas.
Hubo un tiempo en que amé lo que escribías,
mezcla vaga de Bécquer con Pizarnik, caligramas o signos descifrables
con sabor a tu cuerpo o su memoria
pero ya no me alienta lo que amamos porque leer ahora es un oficio muerto.
Y habré de conformarme con tus palabras tristes, que ya son
para otro, un fraude en el silencio, sediciosas palabras, acídulas,
protervas, como el alma podrida de una semilla rancia.

The Bad Poem

Translation by Sarah E. Blanton

> *Live in a barrel.*
> *Break your head with a hatchet.*
> *Plant tulips in the rain.*
> *But don't write poetry.*
> *Bukowski*

Perhaps we dare
—perhaps to confront the infinite world—
        to be another way,
to leave the skin of the self in the other when to the zeal of death
we cling.
We are so defenseless under the tense nakedness that carves us,
under the tremor that blinds
the rivers of blood, the flower of such nerve whose strange vision
obscures.
And you keep writing love like nothing,
As if raw time that whittles us down and leaves me hanging in the
open
were not more than oblivion or more than shadow.
Would you be sure to write me when you write love if you would
understand the pain that your words distill,
the pain that it costs me to receive them.
There was a time when I loved what you wrote,
vague mixture of Bécquer with Pizarnik, calligrams or
decipherable signs
with the taste of your body or its memory
but what we loved no longer inspires me because reading is a dead
trade.
And I will have to settle for your sad words, that are for another
now, a fraud in silence, seditious words, acidulous, perverse, like
the rotten soul of a rancid seed.

Quieres que te recuerde como un dios ofendido, náufrago de tus risas, de tus rosas y labios, lamiendo las promesas de unos besos furtivos que albergaron demonios y apagaron el fuego. De qué sirven ahora cuando la luz es noche, cuando un sueño te nubla y un vacío te sustenta, y es un dedal la lumbre donde tu voz columbra. Si vuelves a escribirme, si yo vuelvo a leerte, no te llames amor, no me confundas. No mezcles lo que fuimos, el oro que licuamos con la savia del vino, la música y el llanto. No traiciones el sueño que en el sueño forjamos, ponte el nombre que quieras, pero no el de poesía.

You want me to remember you as an offended god, shipwrecked
by your laughter, your roses and lips, licking the promises of a few
furtive kisses that harbored demons and extinguished fire.
What good are they now when the light is night,
when you are clouded by a dream and sustained by an emptiness,
there's a thimble of flame where your voice gleams.
If you write me again, if I read you again, do not call yourself love,
don't confuse me.
Don't mix what we were, the gold that we liquified with the sap of
wine, the music and the cry. Don't betray the dream that within
the dream we forged, give it the name you want, but not poetry.

La madre desguazada

Short story by Lourdes García Pinel

A nuestra madre le gustaba mirarse en los espejos, hasta que un día se le desprendió un brazo. Llegó rodando hasta nuestros pies, con la mano extendida en actitud mendicante. Mi hermana y yo permanecimos la una frente a la otra, observando el resto de mamá sobre el piso, y como somos gemelas, cuando alzamos la vista, por un momento creímos estar viendo nuestro reflejo. Nos palpamos, y al comprobar que no faltaba nada, comprendimos. No éramos nosotras, era mamá.

Mi hermana sumergió el brazo dentro de un cuenco con agua. "A lo mejor, le crecen flores", dijo, y entonces el brazo se dio la vuelta: ahora parecía la garra de una cría de monstruo.

Mamá seguía mirándose en los espejos, así que pronto la casa se fue llenando de más cuencos con agua, de los que nunca crecía nada, ni siquiera unas ramitas.

"¿Y si escondemos los espejos?", propuso mi hermana. Pero, ay, también estaban los ventanales, la cubertería de plata, las lámparas de cristal. Fue así cómo se le desprendieron los ojos: subida a un taburete, haciendo equilibrios sobre su única pierna, mientras limpiaba la araña del salón. No nos dimos cuenta de lo bellos que eran hasta que los tuvimos entre nuestras manos.

Cuando no cupieron más cuencos en las habitaciones, llevamos todos los miembros en una carretilla a la parte trasera de la casa. "Quizá aquí sí le crezcan flores", dijo mi hermana con un tono descorazonador contemplando la tierra seca, pero en ese momento nuestra mirada se encontró, y nos vimos reflejadas. Entonces cavamos hondo, todo lo hondo que pudimos y los sepultamos en lo más profundo de aquella tierra seca, como quien entierra un recuerdo funesto.

The Scrapped Mother

Translation by Maya Vinuesa

Our mother liked to look at herself in mirrors, until the day one of her arms fell off. It rolled toward our feet with the palm extended in a gesture of begging. My sister and I stood facing each other, watching Mum's remainders on the ground. We were twins, so when we looked up, we thought we were seeing our own reflection. We felt one another and, once we had checked that there was nothing missing, we understood.

My sister plunged the arm into a bowl filled with water. "Maybe flowers will grow from it," she said. And then the arm turned around—now it resembled the paw of a monster's pup. Mum went on looking at herself in mirrors, so that soon the house was filled with bowls of water where nothing grew, not even little branches.

"What if we hid the mirrors?" suggested my sister. Oh, but there were also those large windows, the silver cutlery, the crystal lamps. That was how her eyes fell out—she was standing on a stool, struggling for balance on her only leg, while she polished the chandelier in the living room. We never realised how beautiful they were until we held them in our hands.

When there was no more space for bowls in the rooms, we put all her body parts into a wheelbarrow and took them to the backyard. "She might grow flowers here," said my sister, gravely disheartened as she beheld the dry land. But our eyes met instantly, and we saw ourselves reflected. We dug deeper and deeper into the ground and we buried them in the depths of that dry land, as someone burying a fateful memory.

La tristeza

Poem by María Marta Guzzetti

La tristeza baja
por una escalera sucia.
En algún lado alguien
escucha un disco rayado.

Hay olor a cebolla
y ese olor de la cebolla
se mezcla con un perfume
inexplicable de violetas.

Baldosas rojas.
Portón de madera oscura
y manijón de hierro.
Yo no subo,
no subiré
por donde baja la tristeza.

Me escapo por un hueco
y trato de esconderme
debajo del felpudo de la entrada.
Pero ella me mira,
distraída
mientras el miedo
se agazapa en mi garganta.

No lloraré.
Solamente cubriré
mis ojos con un cristal oscuro.
Y la próxima vez
evitaré entrar en casas
como esta

Sadness

Translation by Ana Grandal

Sadness climbs down
a dirty staircase.

Somewhere someone
listens to a scratched record.

It smells like onions
and that smell of onions
mixes with an inexplicable
scent of violets.

Red floor tiles.
Dark wooden door
and large iron knob.
I do not climb up,
I will not climb up
where sadness climbs down.

I escape through a gap
and try to hide
beneath the doormat at the entrance.
But she glances at me
absently,
while fear
crouches in my throat.

I won't cry.
I will only cover
my eyes with a dark glass.
And the next time
I'll avoid coming inside houses
like this one

donde alguien ha llorado
cebolla
y algún otro
ha perdido
ese perfume de violetas.

where someone has cried
onions
and somebody else
has lost
that scent of violets.

Garzas Blancas *

Poem by Mertxe Manso

Derrama el corazón
por la rivera
allí donde fluye el agua
que se vierta
fluye vida,
se derrama el cielo
mira,
laten los sentidos
fluyen por la judería
somos aire,
tú, tormenta
yo, lluvia.
Si se rompen
las nubes
que se derramen
entre las flores del sol,
allí, donde el botánico,
guarda los sabores.
Ruge el molino de regolfo,
eres batán que golpea,
yo aceña que te para.
En los nidos duermen
garzas, somos libres
para sentirnos
mientras nace el alba
y se refleja en ti.

* This poem will be published in the collection *Mirlos blancos* (2021).

White Herons

Translation by Meaghan Coogan

Spill your heart
into the riverbank
where the water flows
let it run
life flows,
the sky is spilling over
look,
the senses pulsate
flowing through the Jewish Quarter
we are air,
you, the storm
I, the rain.
If the clouds
break apart,
let them spill
among the sun's flowers,
there, where the garden
keeps the fragrances.
The mill bellows,
You are the pounding churn,
I, the water wheel that stops you.
In the nests sleep
herons, we are free
to feel each other
as the dawn is born
and is reflected in you.

Cerrojos a los parques

Poem by Sara Medina

Y dice que ya no ama,
que pone empeño;
¿acaso pretende amasar el cielo
con asfalto y semáforos?

Pues somos arenas movedizas –dice–,
vencejos moribundos,
perros enclenques.

Porque insiste
en que somos playas
atestadas de niños
cayendo por toboganes.

Y yo nos veo más bien
como a un océano bailando
en una jaula.

Locking Parks

Translation by Ana Grandal

And he says he loves no more,
that he keenly tries;
does he expect to knead the sky
with asphalt and traffic lights?

For we are quicksand
—he says—
dying swifts,
lank dogs.

Because he insists
that we are beaches
cluttered with children
slipping down slides.

And I rather see ourselves
like an ocean dancing
in a cage.

¿Qué fue de aquellos personajes?

Poem by Mario Meléndez

Alicia en el país de …

Mientras torturaban al Lirón
la niña pensó que pronto llegaría su hora

Sintió los gritos del Sombrerero Loco
en la sala contigua

Reconoció el cadáver de La Liebre
apilado sobre otros cuerpos

Oyó a la Reina de Corazones
confesar al oído del verdugo

Y a la madre del Conejo Blanco
repetir algunos nombres extraños

Todo sucedía en cámara lenta
como la noche que Dios falleció

Muerte de Caperucita

La torturaron hasta en el más allá

Nunca dijo dónde estaba El Lobo
tampoco La Abuelita

Fue arrojada a la fosa con Pinocho
Alicia, El Gato con Botas

Nadie escribió siquiera un epitafio

What Became of Those Characters?

Translation by Mireya Jamal

Alice in Wonder...

While they tortured Dormouse
the girl thought her hour would come soon

She felt the screams of the Mad Hatter
in the other room

She recognized the Hare's corpse
piled on top of other bodies

She heard the Queen of Hearts
confess in the executioner's ear

And the White Rabbit's mother
repeating a few strange names

Everything was happening in slow motion
like the night God died

Death of Little Red Riding Hood

They tortured her even in the afterlife

She never said where the Wolf was
or Grandma

She was thrown into the mass grave with Pinocchio
Alice, Puss in Boots

No one even wrote an epitaph

Ahora es detenida desaparecida
al igual que Dios

La bella durmiente

Despertará si la besa el verdugo
si la besan los torturados
que escriben en los muros
           venceremos

Despertará con los ojos llorosos
quejándose del golpe en las costillas
la mandíbula rota
      la corona de espinas

O se irá simplemente en el sueño
remando en un mar de desaparecidos
que la llaman desde el fondo
cantando
    venceremos

Blancanieves

Lo primero llegando al cementerio
fue buscar la tumba de Blancanieves
pero sólo halló una fosa clandestina
donde habían enterrado a los enanos

(Esto escribía la niña en su diario de muerte
cuando le avisaron que sus muñecas
no vendrían a visitarla)

She is now among the detained and disappeared
just like God

Sleeping Beauty

She will awaken if kissed by the executioner
if kissed by those tortured
who write on walls
                    we will prevail

She will awaken teary eyed
complaining about the blow to her ribs
her broken jaw
                    crown of thorns

Or she'll simply go in her sleep
rowing in a sea of those missing
calling to her from the depths
singing
            we will prevail

Snow White

First thing upon arriving to the cemetery
she searched for Snow White's tomb
but she only found a clandestine grave
where the dwarves were buried

(A girl was writing this in her death diary
when she was told her dolls
would not come to visit)

Enfermera

Poem by Rodrigo Montera

Después de sonreír,
la enfermera dijo:

Hay que elegir por qué llorar.

Yo, por ejemplo,
ya no lloro por mis salas de emergencia,
tampoco
por las jaulas de los tigres
o por el insomnio que me ocasionan
los sueños de los niños.

No lloro
por las películas violentas
protagonizadas
por aves o asesinos,
ni por las novelas
que no han descrito
el dolor de los naranjos.

Y desde hace tiempo,
y de esto me enorgullezco particularmente,
dejé de llorar
por los muelles
atados a los barcos,
por las señales de tránsito en desuso,
y por las mujeres que confunden
su corazón con un florero.

Tampoco lloro por los deportes que no aprendí.
Ni por los días
que uso

The Nurse

Translation by Olga Yudenkova

After smiling,
the nurse said:

One must choose the reasons to cry.

I, for example,
no longer cry for my emergency rooms.
Neither do I cry
for the cages with the tigers in them,
nor for the sleeplessness
that children's dreams bring about.

I do not cry
because of the violent movies
that feature
birds or killers,
nor do I cry for the novels
that haven't described
the pain of the orange trees.

Since long ago,
and this makes me particularly proud,
I've stopped crying
for the piers
that are tied to the boats,
for the road signs that have fallen into disuse
and for women who mistake
a heart for a vase.

Neither do I cry for sports I haven't learned,
nor for the days
when I use

un nuevo perfume
sin que nadie
se dé cuenta.

Y no, no lloro por el mar.

Yo
elegí llorar
por los hombres
que no saben describir un círculo,
por los juguetes
que no recogieron a sus dueños,
por las escaleras
que no pueden subir los mutilados.

Decidí llorar
por las abuelas
que confunden
sus recetas
con sus recuerdos
y saborean en silencio
y como un mendrugo
las fotografías de sus nietos;
lloro por los zapatos de las dependientas
en Nochebuena
y por cada una
de las casas
que no supe abandonar.

Pero por lo que no
elegí llorar
aquello por lo que lloro
sin que pueda controlarme
es por las mujeres que,
repentinamente,
dejan de bailar.

a new perfume
without anyone
noticing it.

And, no, I do not cry for the sea.

I
choose to cry
for men
who do not know how to describe a circle,
for the toys
that do not put away their owners,
for the stairs
that cannot be used by those who are crippled.

I've chosen to cry
for grandmas
who confuse
their recipes
with their memories
and enjoy in silence,
as if it were their bread,
the photographs of their grandkids' faces.
I cry for the shoes of the saleswomen
on Christmas Eve
and for each
of the houses
that didn't know how to leave.

But for every reason
I choose not to cry for,
there's something for which,
without any control,
I cry.
I do cry for women who
suddenly

Por eso,
por más que me lo pidan
mi sombra y mis amigos
a solas

nunca bailo
conmigo.

stop dancing.

That's why
no matter how much my shadow and my friends beg me,
when I'm alone

I never dance
with myself.

Investigación

Poem by Rodrigo Montera

Investigo la imaginación,
dijo la mujer en el museo,
después dio un sorbo a su bebida.

Yo tuve deseos de preguntarle
si su investigación
incluía el mar,
o si existía alguna teoría
que afirmara
que el océano
es una flecha
que apunta
a la memoria.

También pensé en preguntarle
por los puntos imaginarios
que observan
las bailarinas
cuando aprenden a dar un giro;
por los pensamientos
de las modelos
en una pasarela;
preguntarle por los pies de dios;
por las rondas infantiles;
y por las ciudades
que no conocen mis padres
y que mis hermanos
y yo
hemos inventado.

De tanto pensar preguntas
no hice ninguna

Research

Translation by Olga Yudenkova.

I study imagination,
said the woman at the museum,
after taking a sip of her drink.

I wanted to ask her
whether her research
included the sea
or whether there was some theory
that confirms
the ocean
to be an arrow
that aims
at the memory.

I also wanted to ask her
about the imaginary spots,
which the dancers
focus on
when they learn how to turn;
about the thoughts
that the models have
while walking down the catwalk;
to ask her about god's feet;
about the children's games;
and about the cities
that my siblings
and I
have made up
but our parents have yet to visit.

From thinking so much,
I didn't ask her any questions

y cuando ella acabó su bebida
intenté abordarla
para descubrir qué sabía
de las tumbas
selladas con nombres falsos;
de los crímenes
que imagina un inocente
una vez que es hallado culpable;
o saber si le interesaban
las obras de arte
que nunca se crearon
por miedo al fracaso.

Anhelé preguntarle
si algún capítulo
de su tesis
abordaba
las mentiras de los niños
o si
el departamento que se encargaba
de dicho tema
era presidido por una niña
que afirmara ser un viejo;
o si tenía algún compañero
que estudiara los goles
que no se anotaron
y que habrían salvado
del descenso
a muchos individuos.

Preguntarle con qué constancia
consultaba el
el diccionario
de palabras inexistentes,
en el que se incluyen
palabras como

and, when she finished her drink,
I tried to approach her
to find out what she knew
about the graves
sealed with false names;
about the crimes
that are imagined by the innocent one
who's found to be guilty;
or maybe she was interested in
works of art
that are never created
due to the fear of failure.

I yearned to ask her
whether any of the chapters
of her thesis
include
the lies of the children
or whether
her thesis supervisor was a girl
who only pretended to be an elder;
or maybe she had a colleague
who studied the goals
not scored
that could have saved
so many fans
from suffering.

To ask her with what consistency
she consulted
the non-existent words dictionary,
which includes
words such as

las *fracasías*
las *hipotercas*
las *melancomías*
los *hombrejueres*
las *mujerembres*
los *tristércoles*
los *migrahambres*
y las *nuvias...*
esas que cuando
llube,
se *escriviven*
los *proemas.*

Preguntarle si
en alguno de sus ensayos
había escrito la palabra aborto;
o si ella me recomendaba
invertir todo mi capital imaginario
en la construcción de una única mentira
o si era mejor
mentir en pequeñas dosis
 a todos aquellos que me preguntaran:
¿Cómo estás?

Antes de despedirse,
ella se fue temprano,
supongo
porque
de noche lleva un registro
de los amores
que no van a ninguna parte,
pensé en preguntarle
si no temía
que su investigación
al final
careciera de imaginación.

failurtasies
motrage
melanchocolate
his-her
her-his
wednesad
hungrants
and *clourains...*
that
rainoud
and *wrilive*
the *proems.*

To ask her whether
in any of her essays
there was the word "abortion" written;
or whether she would recommend to me
investing all of my imaginary capital
into constructing one big lie,
or whether it would be better
to lie in small doses
to all those who ask me:
"How are you?"

She left early,
before saying goodbye.
I suppose
The night has brought up the records
of those love interests
that go nowhere.
I wanted to ask her
if she wasn't scared
that, at the end of it all,
her research
just lacked imagination.

La epifanía de los semáforos

Poem by Rafael Núñez

Veis ahí todos esos edificios: serán escombros,
un escape roto. El brillo de sus caras,
todas serán un crepúsculo robado por la muerte.
La vida comienza a terminar, ya no te atrae el fulgor,
la rabia y el estrepito. Los cristales te muestran,
que debes empezar desde el lado real de la imagen.
Falso reflejo de ti mismo, hay en un charco
de agua sucia por las botas de dos jóvenes,
que gritan sin saber que la muerte viene.
La juventud se marcha al mismo tiempo,
que esas dos cruzan la acera. Ilusas, sí,
pero ya no formas parte de su mundo.
Date cuenta, mira al suelo, todavía caminas
por encima de las hojas caídas, todavía,
no las miras. No eres tan joven como querrías,
y tienes miedo de serlo y perderte de ese viaje
tan largo como de la nada hacia la nada.
De eso trata la vida. Debes saberlo, la juventud
un charco sucio y pasajero,
tu solo tenías derecho a saltar sobre tu reflejo
antes que el semáforo se ponga en rojo
o deje de funcionar la electricidad de sus pupilas.

The Traffic Light Epiphany

Translation by Katelyn Smith

You see all of those buildings there: they will be rubble,
a broken escape. The glow of their faces,
all will be a twilight stolen by death.
Life begins to end, now you're not attracted by radiance,
rage, pandemonium. The looking glass shows you,
that you should start from the real side of the image.
A false reflection of yourself lies in a puddle
of water, dirty from the boots of two young women
who shout without knowing that death is coming.
Youth marches at the same time,
as those two cross the sidewalk. They're naive, yes,
but now you're no longer part of their world.
Wake up, look at the ground, you still walk
over the fallen leaves, still,
you don't look at them. You're not as young as you'd like to be,
and you're afraid to be and to miss out on that trip
as long as from nothing to nothingness.
This is what life's about. You should know that, youth
a dirty and passing puddle,
only you had the right to jump over your reflection
before the traffic light turns red
or the electricity of your pupils stops working.

Café veneto

Poem by Rafael Núñez

Remuévelo con cuidado,
no provoques el caos.
Qué oscuros haces los conciertos,

que saben a soledad y abrigo.
Los viajes hasta Castello,
las derrotas brillantes de las máscaras en san Marcos.
Mueve el café con cuidado,
quizá el cielo guarde algo para ti.

El café frío como cóctel
muerto sobre tu garganta,
Bebe con cuidado, no te llamen

los santos de Venezia a que bailes
la peste que ahora llamamos olvido.

Venetian Coffee

Translation by Katelyn Smith

Stir with care,
don't provoke chaos.
For you make the concerts dark,
that taste of solitude and refuge.

The trips down to Castello,
the brilliant loss of masks in San Marcos.
Stir the coffee with care,
maybe heaven keeps something for you.
The cold coffee like a cocktail
dead against your throat,
drink with care so they don't call you

the saints of Venice for whom you dance
the plague that we now call oblivion.

De un cielo a otro

Poem by Viviana Paletta

> *Una gota de sangre cae de un cielo a otro,*
> *deslumbrante.*
>
> Victor SERGE, *Manos*

1

Como una grieta
fumea
la mirada.
Baraja su astilla
clavada de luz.

No hay nadie
en las arterias.

Los aviones laminan
el cielo del Jarama
seco, trigueño, traslúcido.

Hay tanto resol
que no se puede tragar.

El frío está lleno
de animales.

Sangre seca en vasijas
sin barro
con la promesa
    de un lago quieto
    de un ancho fruto.

From One Sky to Another

Translation by Carola Aikin and Nadine Novack

> *A drop of blood falls from one sky to another,*
> *dazzling.*
> *Victor SERGE, Hands*

1

Like a crack
fumes
the stare.
Shuffles its splinter
stabbed by light.

There is no one
in the arteries.

Airplanes laminate
the Jarama river sky
dry, wheaten, translucent.

So much brightness
is hard to swallow.

The chill is full
of animals.

Dry blood
in clayless jars
with the promise
        of a quiet lake
        of ample fruit.

2

Nadie alcanza
el anzuelo en la orilla.

Peces agrietados
de frío
y superficie.

Gemas salobres
embarradas
que flaquean
en los cauces sin recodos
de la meseta.

El esqueleto permanece
de pie en el enjambre de los alisios
con plumas de sol en el pelo
tornasoladas
invisibles.

3

Astillados vocablos
gritería muda.

Un aljibe hundido:
atribulada raíz
sin tallo, nada verdea
(ningún brote).

Millones de seres
semejantes
a enramadas secas
que no hacen sombra
bajo su pie.

2

No one reaches
the hook on the river bank.

Fish crackled
		by cold
		and surface.

Salty gems
muddied
that flounder
in riverbeds without bends
on the plateau.

The skeleton remains
standing in the swarm of trade winds
with sunny feathers in its hair
			iridescent
			invisible.

3

Splintered phrases
		mute clamor.

A sunken cistern:
troubled root
without stem, no greenery
(not a bud).

Millions of beings
similar
to dry arbor
cast no shadows
underfoot.

Piedras mis padres
piedras mi casa
piedras la tumba
para esta extensión de huesos
    y su soniquete de tinaja
    y su reguero de pólvora.

4

Uno es otro
    irremediablemente
a un lado y al otro
del cielo.

Llamaradas hermanas
vienen a abrevar
en la noche
del nopal.

Todos interiores
los mares de este pedrusco
terrestre.

Cuatrocientos millones lo cruzarán
a dentelladas
    de sueñera
    y olvido.

No se sale ileso
de la travesía
demorada el alma
el hambre inclinada
cumplido el tiempo.

5

Soplamos escamas
de peces andinos.

Stones my parents
stones my home
stones the tomb
for this extension of bones
        and its rattling clay urn
        and its gunpowder trail.

4

One is the other
        hopelessly
on one side and another
of the sky.

Sibling flames
drink at the trough
in the night
of the Nopal.

All are inland
the seas of this terrestrial
boulder.

Four hundred million will cross it
bite by bite
        of dreaminess, *sueñera*,
        and oblivion

Nobody comes out unharmed
from the crossing
the soul delayed
to hunger inclined
the time spent.

5

We blow scales
of Andean fish

Flamean un instante
en el aire.

Un cuenco de ruido
abriga el costillar.

Se rumia el paisaje
de memoria errónea.
Cortejo de migrantes
sin exequias
para encender una vida con otra
con pétalos de cal.

El frío está lleno de animales.

No hay atajo
en la noche cuántica.

flash for an instant
in the air.

A crock of noise
shelters the ribcage.

The landscape is ruminated
by erroneous memories.
Entourage of migrants
with no rituals
to light up one life with another
with lime petals.

The chill is full of animals.

There is no shortcut
In the quantic night.

Tauromaquia *

Short story by Carmen Peire

Es la hora del paseíllo, le dijeron cuando abrió la puerta. Y el monosabio se puso el uniforme, pantalón oscuro, blusón rojo, gorrilla del mismo color. Pensando en su trabajo en el ruedo durante la lidia, él, que ayudaba al picador, que podía pisar la arena junto a los toreros, salió de casa a cumplir con su destino, extrañado de que fueran a buscarlo en una fría noche sin luna.

Falta de reflejos *

Short story by Carmen Peire

No te escaparás tan rápido, me dijo desde fuera impidiendo la salida.
No despertarás tan pronto, me dijo desde dentro anulando mi sueño.
No te saldrás con la tuya, dijo desde arriba con su bota en mi garganta.
No sabrás el suelo que pisas, gritó desde abajo removiendo mis cimientos.
Cuando quise enfrentarme, estaba rodeada.

* These poems were originally published in *Horizonte de sucesos* (2011).

Bullfighting

Translation by Carola Aikin

It's time for *El paseíllo*, the ceremonial entry into the arena, they told him when he opened the door. And the picador's assistant, the *monosabio*, put on his uniform: dark trousers, red blouse, a cap of the same color. Thinking about his task in the arena during the bullfight he —who assisted the picador, he, who could tread the same soil as the bullfighters —, left his home to fulfill his destiny, somewhat puzzled that they should come to fetch him on a cold moonless night.

Lack of Reflexes

Translation by Carola Aikin

You won't escape so quickly, he said from the outside, blocking the way out.

You won't wake up so soon, he said from the inside, aborting my dream.

You won't get your way, he said from above with his boot on my throat.

You won't distinguish the soil on which you tread, he cried from below, shaking my foundations.

When I wanted to confront him, I was surrounded.

Las lenguas curiosean *

Poem by Marta Sanz

Las lenguas curiosean
y les gusta decir siempre
la última palabra,
gobernadoras,
sin lenguaje,
sólo húmedo
cerco
de carne
roja.

* This poem was originally published in the collection *Hardcore* (2010)

The Tongues Poke Around

Translation by Sam Krieg

The tongues poke around
and they always like to say
the last word,
governors,
without language,
just a wet
fence
of red
meat.

No quiero la palabra precisa *

Poem by Marta Sanz

No quiero la palabra precisa.
Es pobre y es pequeña.
Quiero una palabra
llena de flecos.
Una lámpara con chupones morados.
Una excrecencia.
Gota que rezuma del canalón.
La estalactita rota.
El polvo de trabajar los brillantes.
Un hielo deshecho.
Y deshaciéndose.
La saliva que le escapa, por la comisura,
a la bella que duerme en el bosque.
La ganga del mineral.
El hilo que sobra detrás del cañamazo.

No quiero la palabra precisa,
sino una llena de flecos,
una lámpara y vuelta a empezar,
un laberinto,
la flor,
una palabra
que ni yo misma entienda
y sólo pueda poseer
cuando los otros,
los de buena voluntad,
me la traduzcan.

* This poem was originally published in *Perra mentirosa* (2010).

I Don't Want the Precise Word

Translation by Sam Krieg

I don't want the precise word.
It's poor and small.
I want a word
full of loose ends.

A lamp with purple suckers.
An excrescence.
A drop that oozes from the gutter.
The broken stalactite.
The dust from cutting diamonds.
Ice shattered.
And melting.
The saliva that escapes, at the corner of her mouth,
from the beauty sleeping in the forest.
The mineral's matrix.
The extra thread behind the canvas.

I don't want the exact word,
but rather one full of loose ends,
a lamp and a restart,
a labyrinth,
the flower,
a word
that not even I would understand
and could only possess
when other people,
those of good will,
translate it for me.

Por el miedo de no ser *

Poem by Marta Sanz

Por el miedo
de no ser
deseada nunca;
por ese miedo
que no es el mismo
que el del ademán,
tan vanidoso,
de una mujer bellísima
–madrastra de Blancanieves,
actriz de cine–
que guarda
sus monedas
en el interior
–vagina, turba humeante–
de su monedero de pellizco
–faltriquera de los triunfos
de una baraja española:
as de oros
tres de bastos–;
por ese miedo
a desaparecer
del azogue
de todos los espejos que,
de pronto,
refulgen desnudos
detrás
de la sábana gris
que los tapaba;
por ese miedo frío
de vieja precoz
o de cadáver

Because of the Fear of Never Being

Translation by Sam Krieg

Because of the fear
of never
being desired;
because of that fear
that is not the same
as that of the expression,
so smug,
of a very beautiful woman
—Snow White's stepmother,
movie actress—
that keeps
her coins
inside
—vagina, steaming peat—
of her change purse
—pocket full of winnings
from a Spanish card game:
Ace of Coins
Three of Wands—;
because of that fear
of disappearing
from the mercury
of all the mirrors that,
suddenly,
glow naked
behind
the gray sheet
that covered them;
because of that cold fear
of woman old before her time
or of a cadaver

que no cumple
su fecha de caducidad,
he dejado
que me besaran
el corazón de la boca:
un loco,
tres enanos saltarines,
los viejos
y varios coleccionistas.

* This poem was originally published in *Vintage* (2013).

that doesn't meet
its expiration date,
I have allowed
them to kiss
deep within my mouth:
a crazy man,
three frolicking dwarves,
old men,
and various collectors.

Las olas chocan

Short story by Carmen Vega

Las olas chocan en la mirada intensa de una superviviente de mil mareas, la mujer, la niña salvaje camina hasta perderse entre árboles que le susurran palabras que sólo ella puede entender. Las horas, los días, los años se suceden entre vientos calientes y helados. Desde mi lejanía oigo su voz y afloran a mi memoria recuerdos borrosos de charlas inacabadas, ahora que los cangrejitos le pican la lengua siente el peso responsable de una soledad atrabiliaria, la pérdida de un amor le atravesó el pensamiento para siempre, la niña mujer salvaje vuela con la ligereza de la golondrina y corre con los cordones de los zapatos mal atados. Amiga aguárdame en el campo de la esperanza y allí esperaremos que el tiempo se vaya desgranando morosamente mientras miramos cómo crecen las camelias.

Waves Clash

Translation by Ana Grandal

Waves crash against the intense gaze of a survivor of a thousand tides, the woman, the wild girl wanders until she loses her way among trees that whisper words only she can understand. Hours, days, years go by between hot and icy winds. From my distance, I hear her voice, and hazy reminiscences of unfinished conversations surface in my memory, now that small crabs prick her tongue she feels the responsible weight of an atrabilious loneliness, the loss of a love pierced her mind forever, the wild woman girl flies with the swallow's nimbleness and runs with loose shoelaces. My friend waits for me in the field of hope and there we will stay as time serenely unstrings itself whilst we watch how camellias grow.

Contributors

The artist

Chema Castelló is a photographer who specializes in architecture, fine arts and portraits, whose work is regularly exhibited in artistic and commercial galleries in Madrid, Spain. We are thankful for his collaboration with *IPR* by providing the cover image for both, our previous and current issues. Information about the artist can be found in https://www.instagram.com/castellochema

DUTCH

Authors

Anna Enquist is the pen name of Christa Widlund-Broer, a renowned pianist and psychoanalyst. Seeking dialogue between the technical and emotional, the poet has found an enormous audience for thirty years now. She is also a widely acclaimed novelist. Anna Enquist lost her daughter in a traffic accident in Dam Square, Amsterdam, in 2001—which led Enquist to battle for blind-spot mirrors on all trucks. In 2003, thanks to her efforts, blind-spot mirrors became compulsory in the Netherlands. Motherhood with children growing up fast and an empty-nest fear are recurring themes in her work, also in this poem.

Leo Vroman was a poet, playwright, artist, and scientist. He was of Jewish descent and a student when World War II broke out. Some days into the war, he said goodbye to his parents, went to the beach of Scheveningen, and managed to reach England on a sailing boat. From there, he travelled on to South-East Asia where he suffered extreme hardships in war camps. After the war he moved to New York and became an American citizen in 1951. He has won almost every Dutch literary poetry prize and is still considered one of the liveliest poets writing in Dutch. Owing to Vroman's light touch, his often-profound subjects easily imprint themselves on the memory. His residence in the United States may have helped him retain the quality of light-footed profundity that has remained untroubled by fashion or trends.

Translator

Arno Bohlmeijer is a poet and novelist, writing in English and Dutch, published in five countries (US: Houghton Mifflin), and in *Universal Oneness: an Anthology of Magnum Opus Poems from around the World*, 2019. Arno is the winner of the Charlotte Köhler Grant, a national oeuvre award, and a PEN America Grant 2021.

ENGLISH-ARABIC

Author/translator

Hasheemah Afaneh is a Palestinian-American writer and public health professional based in New Orleans. Some of her work has appeared in *Sinking City Literary Magazine, 580 Split Magazine, Glass Poetry Poets Resist Series, Poets Reading the News*, and *This Week in Palestine*. More information about the author can be found at norestrictionswords.wordpress.com. She tweets @its_hashie.

ENGLISH

Authors

Alan Cohen was a poet before beginning his career as a Primary Care MD, teacher, and manager. He has been writing poems for 60 years and is beginning now to share some of his discoveries. He has been married to Anita for 41 years, and for the last 11, they have lived in Eugene, Oregon.

Stuart Gunter lives in Schuyler, Virginia. His poems have been published in *Poet Lore, Hiram Poetry Review, Appalachian Journal, James Dickey Review, Cold Mountain Review,* and *Plume.*

Cindy King is an Assistant Professor of Creative Writing at Dixie State University and editor of *The Southern Quill.* She also enjoys serving on the artistic board for the Blank Theatre in Hollywood, California and writing screen scripts for their Living Room Series. She has been awarded a Tennessee Williams Scholarship and has received the Agha Shahid Ali Scholarship in Poetry from the Fine Arts Work Center in Provincetown. She is the author of *Zoonotic* (2021) and *Easy Street* (2021).

Tim Mayo has published two full-length collections of poetry, *The Kingdom of Possibilities* (2008) and *Thesaurus of Separation* (2016), which was a finalist for both the 2017 Montaigne Medal and the 2017 Eric Hoffer Book Award. His most recent collection, *Notes to the Mental Hospital Time Keeper* (2019) won Honorable Mention in the 2020 Eric Hoffer Book Awards. A seven-time Pushcart Prize nominee, he also is a founding member of the Brattleboro Literary Festival in Vermont.

Gordon E. McNeer is a Professor in the Department of Spanish and Portuguese at the University of North Georgia. He is the translator and editor of *Poetry Facing Uncertainty* (2012), *Shelter from the Storm* (2013), and *Eyes of the Pelican* (2013). He is the author of *Mira lo que has hecho* (2014) and *Poems from Walden* (2021).

David Schenck is the former Director of Ethics at the Medical University of South Carolina. He is the co-author of *Healers: Extraordinary Clinicians at Work and What Patients Teach.* Now retired, he enjoys writing poetry.

Karis Taylor is an undergraduate student at The University of North Carolina, Greensboro.

Authors

Irene Moccia was the recipient of the Carlo Levi Poetry Prize in 2019. She has performed her poetry, which focuses on female identity, body consciousness, and the magic of the mundane, in various festivals throughout Italy. She holds a Law degree and is currently working as Human Resources legal counsel in an insurance company. Her project *Ritenzione lirica* aims to disseminate poetry on social media.

Stefano De Vecchi works in hospice. "Poesia di non amore" is his first poem to be published. He likes taking strolls, playing soccer, and going to the library to write down anything that inspires him.

Translator

Rose Facchini is a Lecturer of Italian Language and Literature at the University of Massachusetts Dartmouth. Her main research focuses on the cultural history of science and technology in Italy through the lens of translated and science fiction. Facchini, whose work has appeared in *Military Medicine*, has participated in the Bread Loaf Translators' Conference and received several fellowships and grants, including the Kathryn Davis Fellowship for Peace and the Katharine Bakeless Nason Endowment. She holds an MA in Italian Literary Studies from the Italian Language School at Middlebury and an MA in International Relations from Salve Regina University.

Authors/Translator

Noemi Alfieri is an Italian researcher based in Portugal since 2014. Both her poetry and research explore borders, gender, violence, and colonialism. *Cem agulhas nos ossos/ Cento aghi nelle ossa* (2020) is her first poetry book. Her poems have appeared in Portuguese and Brazilian literary journals; her non-academic essays, in Italian magazines; and her academic publications in a variety of venues.

Translator

Alexis Levitin has published forty-five books in translation, mostly poetry from Portugal, Brazil, and Ecuador. In addition to three books by Salgado Maranhão, his translations include Clarice Lispector's *Soulstorm* and Eugénio de Andrade's *Forbidden Words*. He has served as a Fulbright Lecturer at universities in Portugal, Ecuador, and Brazil.

Author

Nora Iuga published her first volume of poems in 1968 and has published books of prose and poetry regularly ever since, receiving many Romanian literary prizes. She has translated many German novels into Romanian, an activity for which she received the prestigious Friedrich Gundolf Prize "for the mediation of German culture abroad."

Translator

Victor Pambuccian is a Professor of Mathematics at Arizona State University. His poetry translations, from Romanian, French, and

German, have appeared in *Words Without Borders, Two Lines, International Poetry Review, Pleiades,* and *Black Sun Lit.* A bilingual anthology of Romanian avant-garde poetry, with his translations, for which he received a 2017 NEA Translation grant, was published in 2018.

SPANISH-ENGLISH

Authors/Translators

Carola Aikin is a short story writer who grew up between Spain and England. She is the author of *Las escamas del dragón* (2005), *Mujer perro* (2012), and *Las primaveras de Verónica* (2018). She translates films and literary texts.

Luis Correa-Díaz is a Professor of Spanish in the Department of Romance Languages at the University of Georgia. His research and teaching interests center on Latin American and Spanish poetry, Critical Theory and Cultural Studies, Human Rights, science and literature, and the Digital Humanities. He is the author of various monographs and edited volumes.

SPANISH

Authors

Sonia Aldama Muñoz (Madrid, 1973) graduated with a double major in Political Science and Sociology. She holds a master's in Creative Writing from Hotel Kafka, Madrid. She teaches narrative and poetry. She has authored three books of poetry: *Cuarto solo (2013), La piel melaza* (2017), and *Sucede la noche (2020).* Other works are included in numerous anthologies.

María Villa Cámara Gómez is a writer with a degree in Business Administration and Management. She was the winner of the literary contest *¿Dónde está la Navidad?* in 2016.

Isabel Cienfuegos is a physician and writer, co-founder of the Association of Women Writers and Illustrators, and co-editor of the anthology of contemporary women writers *Esas que también soy yo. Nosotras escribimos* (2019). Her short stories have appeared in numerous anthologies and in national and international literary magazines. She is the author *Mañana los amores serán rocas* (2012) and *Puntos de luz en la noche* (2019). She is a Setenil Award finalist.

María Luisa Cortés is a visual artist who has shown her portraits in several exhibitions. She has participated in numerous creative writing workshops. Her Meniere's syndrome has rendered her severely deaf. She is co-author of her memoir *Vértigo* about living with this condition. One of her images is included after her poem.

Bárbara Darder left her job in finance to fully dedicate herself to writing. Darder is the author of *Mejor Púgil que Tahúr,* (2011), *Espejos de Feria* (2015), *El Edicto* (2019), and *¿Dónde está Sirio, mamá?* (2021).

Mónica Gabriel y Galán is a poet from Madrid, who has lived in Toledo, Miami, and Buenos Aires. She grew up surrounded by music and literature, studied at the Royal Conservatory of Madrid, and was once a pop singer. Gabriel y Galán has published four poetry collections. She has been awarded several poetry awards, two national prizes among them. She is cofounder and active participant of a creative copywriting and editing agency.

Manuel Gahete is a Professor of Language and Literature, vice-president of the Royal Academy of Córdoba (Spain), and president of the Andalucía Chapter of the Association of Writers in Spain, whose works *Nacimiento al amor* (1985), *Capítulo del* (1988), *Íntimo cuerpo sin luz* (1990), *La región encendida* (2000), *Mapa físico* (2002), *El legado de arcilla* (2004), *Mitos urbanos* (2007), *El fuego en* *la ceniza* (2013), and *Los reinos solares* (2014) have received numerous awards.

Lourdes García Pinel is a journalist and a schoolteacher. Her stories have appeared in literary magazines and anthologies such as *Habitación 201, Antología de microrrelatos eróticos,* and *Esas que también soy yo.*

María Marta Guzzetti is a visual artist, poet, and short story writer. Her work frequently explores the female universe. She finds inspiration in dialoguing with women from different cultures, ages, and conditions. Her literary work has been published in Italy and Spain.

Mertxe Manso received a Law degree from the University of Córdoba, Spain. She is a currently a Professor of Spanish Language and Literature. She is the author of *Diario de los cuerpos* (2004), *Tabla de mareas* (2004), *Reglas de navegación* (2006), *Ferronerie* (2009), *Canela picante* (2013), and *Bicicletas en invierno* (2018), which has received numerous awards.

Sara Medina is a poet and a playwright. She teaches Creative Writing in Spain. She has written and directed two plays based on her poetic texts—*Todo mi amor en una noche* and *Sci Vivere.* She is the author of *Como arderá la niebla* (2015). Her poems are published in various anthologies and literary journals.

Mario Meléndez is a writer with a degree in Journalism from the Universidad de Santiago, Chile. He is the author of *Autocultura y juicio* (1994), *Apuntes para una leyenda* (2002), and *Vuelo subterráneo* (2005). His poems have appeared in various literary journals and anthologies. He is the recipient of the Harvest International Award granted by the Polytechnic University of California.

Rodrigo Montera has a bachelor's degree in Literature and Creative Writing from the Cultural Center Casa Lamm (Mexico). He has worked as a teacher, editor, and theatre director. Currently he is working on a documentary about artistic education and mediation for the Museum Consortium of Valencia.

Rafael Núñez Rodríguez is a doctoral candidate at The University of North Carolina at Chapel Hill. He has published the *Antología de poesía joven Onubense* (Niebla, 2016). In addition, he has published articles on contemporary poetry about authors such as José Eugenio Sánchez and Karmelo Iribarren. He also co-hosted a radio program on contemporary poetry called *La arcadia onubense.*

Viviana Paletta received in 1986 the first prize for Poetry at the Frist Library Contest for Argentine Women, and in 1989 her short stories and poetry were featured at the Frist Biennial of Young Art in Argentina. She is the author of *El patrimonio del aire* (2003) and *Las naciones hechizadas* (2010 and 2017), and *Arquitecturas fugaces* (2018). Her poems are included in several anthologies.

Carmen Peire is the founder and president of AMEIS (Association of Women Writers and Illustrators). She has authored three collections of short stories, *Principio de incertidumbre* (2006), *Horizonte de sucesos* (2011), and *Cuestión de tiempo* (2017), and a novel, *En el año de Electra* (2014). She has co-edited the anthology *Esas que también soy yo. Nosotras escribimos* (2019).

Carmen Vega studied drama and cinematography. She works in the film industry as a producer, distributor, exhibiter, reviewer, and historian. Her books are *La navaja de Buñuel* (2008) and *Cuaderno de conversación* (2018). Her short stories and poems have appeared in various books and journals.

Marta Sanz is a Spanish writer with thirteen published novels, among them *Los mejores tiempos* (2001), *Susana y los viejos* (2006), *Daniela Astor y la caja negra* (2013), *Farándula*, which won the 2015 Premio Herralde, and *Pequeñas mujeres rojas* (2020). She is also a poet; among her notable works is the award-winning collection *Vintage* (2013).

Translators

Sarah E. Blanton is a doctoral student specializing in Latin American Literature in the Department of Romance Studies at The University of North Carolina at Chapel Hill. She is interested in migration narratives, translation, and historical memory.

Meaghan Coogan is a PhD student in the Department of Romance Studies at The University of North Carolina at Chapel Hill. Her research focuses on Afro-diasporic literary and artistic expression in the Hispanophone and Francophone Caribbean and how coloniality manifests itself through pathways of migration between the Caribbean and its former colonial powers and current neocolonial powers. In 2020 she received a FLAS fellowship to study Haitian Creole at Duke University.

Ana Grandal is a translator and the author of the flash fiction trilogy *Destroyer*, which includes *Te amo, destrúyeme* (2015), *Hola, te quiero, ya no, adiós* (2017), and *Microsexo* (2019). She has co-edited the collection of short stories *La vida es un bar* (2016). She contributes to e-zines such as *La Charca Literaria* and *La Ignorancia*.

Mireya Jamal grew up on the U.S.-Mexico border with her time spent between the sister cities of Brownsville and Matamoros. She is a graduate student at The University of North Carolina at Chapel Hill, interested in gender and sexuality studies, border studies, and identity. Her interest in translation is deeply rooted in the borderlands she calls home.

Nadine Novack is an illustrator, currently exploring the 3D Digital Sculpture environment. She works as a Spanish/English translator for film and fiction publications.

Sam Krieg received his doctorate in Spanish in 2020 from The University of North Carolina at Chapel Hill, where he is currently Assistant Teaching Professor of Spanish. His research interests focus mainly on literature from the Spanish viceroyalties. His publications can be found in *Dieciocho*, *South Atlantic Review*, and elsewhere.

Katelyn Smith is a PhD student at The University of North Carolina at Chapel Hill. She is specializing in twentieth- and twenty-first-century Latin American narrative. Her current interests include contemporary Indigenous Literatures, ecofeminist theory, gender and sexuality studies, and translation studies. She also teaches undergraduate Spanish language and culture courses as a Graduate Teaching Fellow at UNC-Chapel Hill.

Maya Vinuesa teaches literary translation in the Department of Modern Philology at the University of Alcalá, Madrid. She has translated narrative written by British, Ghanaian, and Nigerian authors. Her first novel is titled *Una habitación en Lavapiés*.

Olga Yudenkova is an ESL instructor from Canada. She has a bachelor's degree in Philosophy and Sociology from University of Alberta. Olga is an aspiring translator who is fluent in four languages and has a great passion for languages and communication.

Books Reviewed

Bautista, Ruperta. *Me'on ts'ibetik/ Letras humildes*. Universidad Nacional Autónoma de México: Publicaciones Fomento Editorial, 2020.

López, Ana Belén. *Ni invisible ni palpable*. Universidad Nacional Autónoma de México: Publicaciones Fomento Editorial, 2020.

Ruiz, Yelitza. *Lengua materna*. Universidad Nacional Autónoma de México: Publicaciones Fomento Editorial, 2020.

The *Dirección de publicaciones y fomento editorial*, connected to the Universidad Nacional Autónoma de México (UNAM), supports the publication of various collections, including *El ala del tigre*, the purpose of which has been to showcase works by contemporary Latin American poets. Among the volumes published in 2020, the books of poems by Ruperta Bautista, Ana Belén López, and Yelitza Ruiz are reviewed here.

The thirty-three bilingual poems (bats'i k'op-Spanish) included in *Me'on ts'ibetik/ Letras humildes* by Ruperta Bautista—a Maya Tsotsil writer, anthropologist, translator, and teacher—reflect upon the themes of resistance and protest. Raising her voice in solidarity, these poems demand social justice as well as the protection of the traditions and lands of indigenous communities. By linking poetry and politics, this collection is a call to action and change on behalf of the indigenous peoples as well as a call to attend to the demands for justice by the families of activists assassinated in Mexico and Honduras. Ana Belén López is a widely-published author, whose recent book of poems, *Ni invisible ni palpable*, explores the tensions between the materiality and immateriality of our embodied lives by transforming sensorial perceptions into non-material understandings of the body. Yelitza Ruiz explores the themes of blood and ancestry, sickness, loss and grieving, language, and the mysteries at the core of the source of life in *Lengua materna*. While focusing on the intimate nature of the feeling of loss, her work mirrors the injustices in today's Mexico and ponders the question of what can be rebuilt from and through what is permanently lost. A lawyer and teacher of art and literature, Ruíz currently leads a research project on women and the Mexican Revolution.

Many thanks to Socorro Venegas, General Director of the *Dirección de publicaciones y fomento editorial* at the UNAM, for sending these volumes to *IPR*, which should become a must-read in courses about contemporary minority writers.

Ana Hontanilla

Books Received

The list acknowledges recent books received by *International Poetry Review*, which may be reviewed at a later date.

Higa, Jeffrey. *Calabash Stories*. University of Central Missouri: Pleiades Press, 2021.

Quiñones, Paige. *The Best Pray*. University of Central Missouri: Pleiades Press, 2021.

Quirarte Vicente. *Bisturí de cuatro filos*. Universidad Nacional Autónoma de México: Publicaciones Fomento Editorial, 2020.

Sánchez, Rodrigo Flores. *Ventana cerrada*. Universidad Nacional Autónoma de México: Publicaciones Fomento Editorial, 2020.

Manuscripts received

Olcina Yuguero, Rebeca. *Cuenticuadros. Cada cuento con su cuadro. Grupo 2. Mata Mua* (seeking publisher). *IPR* acknowledges receipt of the manuscript *Mata Mua*, a creative rewriting of a foundational myth of Tahitian society from a feminist perspective. The stories are illustrated with Paul Gauguin's paintings during his trip to Tahiti.

CPSIA information can be obtained
at www.ICGtesting.com
Printed in the USA
LVHW071539010921
696697LV00019B/1996

9 781469 668574